I Am Autism I Am Autism I Am Autism

Jimmy Huston

ISBN: 978-1-965153-64-2

Cosworth Publishing
21545 Yucatan Avenue
Woodland Hills CA 91364
www.cosworthpublishing.com

Dedicated

I get right to the point.

I know I’m different.

So what?

I'm not dumb.

Speaking can be hard for me.

Let's find another way.

Eye contact is stupid.

But I'll try.

I don't like loud noises.

They hurt.

I think differently.

But I'm not wrong.

I'm not mad at you.

I'm frustrated.

Don’t touch me.

My skin is more sensitive than yours.

It hurts.

Leave me alone.

I'm interested in something else.

Don't be surprised when I surprise you.

Maybe I have nothing to say.

I'm thinking.

I will calm down.

Scolding me doesn't help.

I can be happy without smiling.

My mind is racing.

Don't make it worse.

You may be right.

But so am I.

I think differently.

But I'm not wrong.

If you're so normal, why can't you understand?

I'm thinking.

Leave me alone.

I am a good worker.

Just give me the right job.

I don't understand.

Can you tell me a different way?

I have an idea.

Let me think.

When you tease me,

it hurts.

Please don't.

Your way isn't the only way.

Let's try mine.

I understand.

I just don't know why it's important.

I don't like hugs.

They aren't the only way to show that I love you.

Yes I do want a family someday.

Tell me before we have to leave.

Give me time to get myself ready.

Use my special interest to teach me things.

I don't mean to be rude.

I just don't get it.

I know when you are laughing at me.

I’m sorry about my temper.

Some things are hard for me.

Autism isn't a curse.

It's an opportunity.

I think differently.

But I'm not wrong.

I know you like it when I smile.

But I don’t know why.

We share some parts of the world.

But not all parts.

Some things fascinate me.

Let me be with them.

Sometimes I just don’t care.

Try again later.

My special interest can lead to a great job.

Eye contact?

And a smile?

Too much.

I would rather be where I am
than where you want me to go.

I don’t like change.

No more changes, please.

Don't even turn the page.

Sometimes there is no middle ground.

Am I being rude?

My feelings don't show on my face.

But I have them.

Some things are very, very interesting to me.

Some things are not.

I can be...

...an engineer.

...a teacher.

...an artist

...a soldier.

...an inventor.

...a parent.

...a musician.

...a farmer.

...a poet.

...a mechanic.

...anything I want to be.

Thank you for your help.

I will succeed.

The End.

Other Books by Jimmy Huston

The I Hate to Read Book

...and I Hate Math 2: Who Needs It?

Nate-Nate the Christmas Snake

The Dyslexic Handbook: Genius Edition

Cussing for Kids!: Etiquette for the Profane

The Attention Deficit Disorder Hyperactive Cookbook: Puzzle Edition

The OCD Funbook: Really?

Autism for Beginners: Surfing the Spectrum

Nuts, Nerds, & Savants: Neurodiversity & Creativity

The Bedtime Book of Bad Dreams: Dozing Dangerously

Baby's First Instruction Manual: How To Be the Center of the Universe

Rat BLEEP and Alien Poop: Not for Parents at All

How to Write This Book: You're Going to Be the Author

The Big Beautiful Book of Burping, Belching, and Barfing

The Book Book: Inside the Inside Story

Why Can't Mommy Spend More Time with Me?

The Amazing, Stupendous, Extraordinary, and Somewhat Unusual SPINNING BOOK: No Batteries Required

That Strange Little Angel

The Snake Test: True? False? Maybe?

Is This Your First Funeral?: A Child's Primer

Don't Go to College, Go to Europe for Less

Dead Is the New Sick: An Insider's Guide to Senility, Paranoia, and Curmudgery

The First Apology Is the Worst: Let's Get It Over With

It's Not Easy Being MISTER Ladybug

www.byjimmyhuston.com
www.cosworthpublishing.com

www.ingramcontent.com/pod-product-compliance
Lightning Source LLC
Chambersburg PA
CBHW042342030426
42335CB00030B/3433
* 9 7 8 1 9 6 5 1 5 3 6 4 2 *